YOUR WORLD OF WORDS

DOVER PUBLICATIONS, INC.
MINEOLA, NEW YORK

Bibliographical Note

Your World of Words, first published by Dover Publications, Inc., in 2015, contains pages from the following online workbooks published by Education.com: *Voracious Vocabulary, Figurative Language, Peter Pan and Neverland,* and *Book Marks the Spot.*

International Standard Book Number

ISBN-13: 978-0-486-80272-5
ISBN-10: 0-486-80272-8

Manufactured in the United States by Courier Corporation
80272801   2015
www.doverpublications.com

CONTENTS

VORACIOUS VOCABULARY

Spelling and Vocabulary Words

Reprint the vocabulary words on the lines provided.

1. abomination: an object or situation that causes displeasure. _____

2. enigmatic: mysterious. _____

3. hypocrite: someone who doesn't practice what they preach. _____

4. livelihood: the way in which someone makes a living. _____

5. madcap: wild or reckless. _____

6. noticeable: obvious, clear, visible. _____

7. exodus: the movement of a group of people to another place. _____

8. balmy: warm, comfortable. Used to describe weather conditions. _____

9. aggressive: angry. _____

10. receipt: the act of accepting something. _____

Find the vocabulary words that fit into these sentences.

"Your chocolate and tuna fish cake recipe is an _____!"

"The temperature in this room is 74 degrees. It's beginning to get quite

_____ in here."

"There was a mass _____ of passengers at the Sunnyvale

train station, leaving me with the train car all to myself."

Spelling and Vocabulary Words

Reprint the vocabulary words on the lines provided

1. **morale:** mood. _____

2. **elaborate:** fancy. _____

3. **lucid:** clear, understandable. _____

4. **liaison:** someone who carries out tasks ordered by another. _____

5. **error:** a mistake. _____

6. **severe:** harsh. _____

7. **decipher:** to decode or make sense of. _____

8. **grief:** extreme sadness, usually at the loss of someone or something. _____

9. **compassion:** empathy. _____

10. **compensate:** to provide something in return for a service. _____

Find the vocabulary words that fit into these sentences.

"I think taking away TV privileges for the week is a rather _____ punishment."

"My teacher didn't show much _____ when I said the dog ate my homework."

"No matter if the team has won or lost, their _____ is always boosted by a pizza party."

3

Spelling and Vocabulary Words

Reprint the vocabulary words on the lines provided.

1. maneuver: a planned movement or strategy. _____

2. saunter: to walk casually, to stroll _____

3. assert: to make a claim. _____

4. garbled: difficult to understand. _____

5. quell: to calm. _____

6. turmoil: confusion. _____

7. wounded: badly injured. _____

8. environment: surroundings. _____

9. derogatory: insulting. _____

10. scientific: related to science. _____

Find the vocabulary words that fit into these sentences.

"He wasn't hurt very badly when he fell down in front of the entire class. Only his pride

was _____."

"Though it's gone down in history as a great moment for all mankind, some people

_____ that the moon landing never happened. "

"My little sister was afraid of going to the dentist, so to _____ her

fears I told her he gives you a new toy when your appointment is over."

Spelling and Vocabulary Words

Reprint the vocabulary words on the lines provided.

1. **nomadic:** moving from place to place. _____

2. **treacherous:** dangerous. _____

3. **ambiance:** surroundings. _____

4. **writhe:** to squirm, wriggle. _____

5. **peaceable:** friendly, calm. _____

6. **loathe:** to hate. _____

7. **eerie:** spooky. _____

8. **dwindle:** to fade out, reach the end. _____

9. **impression:** indentation or mark left behind by a person or thing. _____

10. **judicial:** related to courts and the law. _____

Find the vocabulary words that fit into these sentences.

"He made a good first _____ by smiling and shaking hands,

but telling me that my tie was ugly made me change my mind about hiring him."

"Walking along the narrow footpath with nothing to stop us from falling off the side of

the cliff seems _____."

"The rain and fog that Halloween night made my neighborhood look _____."

Spelling and Vocabulary Words

Reprint the vocabulary words on the lines provided.

1. **negotiate:** to bargain with another person. _____

2. **urgent:** of great importance, must be completed in a timely manner. _____

3. **fascinating:** very interesting. _____

4. **subside:** to slowly fade or quiet down. _____

5. **conserve:** to use less of something in order to save it. _____

6. **reserved:** quiet, shy. _____

7. **vagabond:** a homeless person. _____

8. **prolong:** to make a period of time longer. _____

9. **parody:** a humorous imitation of a person, place, or thing. _____

10. **medieval:** related to medieval times. _____

Find the vocabulary words that fit into these sentences.

"This old piece of dental equipment looks like a _____ torture device."

" I watched the clock as it got closer to the end of class, but that only seemed

to _____ the bell. "

" I am insulted by your _____ of me. I do not have a squeaky voice!"

Spelling and Vocabulary Words

Reprint the vocabulary words on the lines provided.

1. **dumbfounded:** shocked, at a loss for words. _____

2. **deceive:** to trick someone or lie to someone on purpose. _____

3. **nonchalant:** casual, unconcerned. _____

4. **valiant:** heroic. _____

5. **savory:** delicious and flavorful, but not sweet. _____

6. **exaggerate:** to make something sound more exciting than it really is. _____

7. **equivalent:** the equal of something. _____

8. **frivolous:** silly, unimportant. _____

9. **waning:** fading. _____

10. **neutral:** undecided, "on the fence". _____

Find the vocabulary words that fit into these sentences.

"At first he made a _____ effort to get the kitten down from the tree, but when she hissed at him he ran away in fright."

"I'm _____ on the issue of cake versus pie."

"My parents say cartoons are _____ but I really like to watch them."

Answers: valiant, neutral, frivolous

Spelling and Vocabulary Words

Reprint the vocabulary words on the lines provided.

1. **intelligent:** smart. _____

2. **repudiate:** to disagree with information you believe is untrue. _____

3. **comprehension:** understanding of a situation. _____

4. **imply:** to hint at something without saying it. _____

5. **realization:** sudden understanding of a situation. _____

6. **coincidence:** a chance meeting or encounter. _____

7. **frumpy:** poor fashion sense, characterized by worn-out or baggy clothing. _____

8. **rhythmic:** something that happens at predictable times. _____

9. **administer:** to give out or dispense something. _____

10. **oaf:** a clumsy person. _____

Find the vocabulary words that fit into these sentences.

"I had a sudden _____ yesterday after looking through all those family

photos . . . you look exactly like your grandfather."

"I will _____ the test on Wednesday. "

"That man's wrinkled sport coat makes him look rather _____ ."

Answers: realization, administer, frumpy

8

Spelling and Vocabulary Words

Reprint the vocabulary words on the lines provided.

1. achievement: something completed successfully. _____

2. undoubtedly: without a doubt, for sure. _____

3. deteriorate: to fall apart, decay. _____

4. option: alternative. _____

5. frustration: a feeling of anxiety and dissatisfaction. _____

6. jealousy: envy. _____

7. Appalachian: A region of the United States in and around the
Appalachian mountain range, or a person who lives in or is from the area. _____

8. ancient: from ancient times. _____

9. digest: to convert food into fuel for the body. _____

10. amnesia: loss of memory. _____

Find the vocabulary words that fit into these sentences.

"I thought I would be a great actor, but when I got up on the stage, I suddenly

had _____ and couldn't remember my lines."

"This _____ computer is so old, it can't connect to the internet."

"Our team will _____ win the science fair if we work together."

Spelling and Vocabulary Words

Reprint the vocabulary words on the lines provided.

1. **reinstate:** to restart a rule or tradition. _____

2. **dictator:** a leader who has total control. _____

3. **sluggish:** slow, lazy. _____

4. **detest:** to be opposed to. _____

5. **tempt:** to tease or entice. _____

6. **famished:** very hungry. _____

7. **acquired:** came into possession of. _____

8. **industrious:** hard-working. _____

9. **monotonous:** repetitive and boring. _____

10. **relent:** to ease up. _____

Find the vocabulary words that fit into these sentences.

"I _____ your decision to put anchovies on that pizza."

"I haven't eaten since this morning. I'm _____ ."

"You've gone from the leader of this group project to a _____ .
None of us have any say in what happens."

Spelling and Vocabulary Words

Reprint the vocabulary words on the lines provided.

1. **taunt:** tease, egg on, make fun of. _____

2. **guarantee:** promise. _____

3. **hoax:** an elaborate prank. _____

4. **exasperate:** to annoy someone. _____

5. **atmosphere:** the air that surrounds the earth. _____

6. **detract:** to take away from something's original meaning. _____

7. **occasion:** an event. _____

8. **appreciate:** to value something. _____

9. **petulant:** impatient, childish. _____

10. **pacify:** to calm someone or something. _____

Find the vocabulary words that fit into these sentences.

"I really _____ my mom's understanding and calm attitude."

"The restaurant's _____ was very casual and relaxed."

"The tale of the 50-foot giant was all a _____ ."

Spelling and Vocabulary Words

Reprint the vocabulary words on the lines provided

1. overthrow: to put a person in charge out of power by force. _____

2. apparel: clothing. _____

3. strapping: powerful, strong. _____

4. contagious: spread by germs. _____

5. stupefy: to stun or shock. _____

6. interval: the "downtime" in between two events or points in time. _____

7. bungle: to mess up. _____

8. essence: a defining characteristic of a person or thing. _____

9. dawdle: to take one's time. _____

10. jargon: slang words and phrases used only in certain groups. _____

Find the vocabulary words that fit into these sentences.

"I couldn't understand what he was saying because he was describing the game

in sports _____ ."

"I need six _____ young men and women to help me move

this furniture. "

"In _____, she is very sweet and good-natured."

Answers: jargon, strapping, essence

12

Spelling and Vocabulary Words

Reprint the vocabulary words on the lines provided.

1. **precede:** to come before. _____

2. **bigot:** a person who shows intolerance toward groups of people they view as different. _____

3. **renowned:** famous, well-respected. _____

4. **consequence:** result. _____

5. **exhausted:** extremely tired. _____

6. **flagrant:** obvious. _____

7. **uncouth:** rude, clumsy, lacking manners. _____

8. **cautious:** careful. _____

9. **chaos:** a state of panic, confusion and/or mayhem. _____

10. **subdued:** relaxed. _____

Find the vocabulary words that fit into these sentences.

" _____ singer Elvis Presley would be in his 70s if he were alive today."

"I'm _____ from all this running around."

"If we remove our famous quadruple-chocolate milkshake from the menu, this town will erupt into _____ ."

13

Spelling and Vocabulary Words

Reprint the vocabulary words on the lines provided.

1. **fidget:** to appear restless or nervous. _____

2. **profound:** significant. _____

3. **antagonist:** the "bad guy" in a story. _____

4. **protagonist:** the "good guy" in a story . _____

5. **nausea:** a feeling of sickness in the stomach. _____

6. **superstitious:** someone who believes in superstition. _____

7. **transient:** doesn't last or stay in one place for long. _____

8. **nostalgia:** a wish to return to a certain time in the past. _____

9. **manipulate:** to operate a device with your hands. _____

10. **prescribe:** to recommend a course of action to someone. _____

Find the vocabulary words that fit into these sentences.

"Hearing that old song puts me in a state of _____ ."

"There was a _____ silence before he started to speak again."

"He's such a strong vegetarian, it gives him _____ to think about eating meat."

Answers: nostalgia, profound, nausea

Spelling and Vocabulary Words

Reprint the vocabulary words on the lines provided.

1. **commission:** a one-time wage paid for a specific service. _____

2. **audition:** to try out or apply for a
certain position, especially in performing arts. _____

3. **recitation:** the recital of something. _____

4. **incorporate:** to include. _____

5. **mischievous:** causes playful, harmless trouble. _____

6. **appropriate:** suitable for a certain use or situation. _____

7. **intercept:** to stop a situation from continuing. _____

8. **prosaic:** dull and boring. _____

9. **upheaval:** a major change. _____

10. **ingenue:** an innocent,
"damsel in distress" character in a book, play or movie. _____

Find the vocabulary words that fit into these sentences.

"Our new puppy is so _____ . I left my sandwich on the counter

for two minutes, and when I came back, he had eaten it!"

"We will _____ your information into our class presentation

as soon as you're finished with it."

"I am such a fan of your work that I'd like to _____ a painting from you."

Answers: mischievous, incorporate, commission

15

Fifth Grade Spelling and Vocabulary Words

Reprint the vocabulary words on the lines provided.

1. shriek: a loud scream. _____

2. strident: loud and annoying. _____

3. inquire: to question. _____

4. wily: clever, tricky. _____

5. tenacious: keeping a strong grip or hold on something. _____

6. depiction: a representation of something. _____

7. ingenious: brilliant, clever. _____

8. disheveled: untidy, messy. _____

9. oasis: a refuge, paradise, or haven. _____

10. persevere: to work hard at a goal. _____

Find the vocabulary words that fit into these sentences.

"The old barn door gave a loud _____ as it was opened for the first time in 50 years."

"With 70 different blends, this new cafe is a coffee-lover's _____."

"She had a _____ grip on his arm during the scary movie."

Double Meaning Words

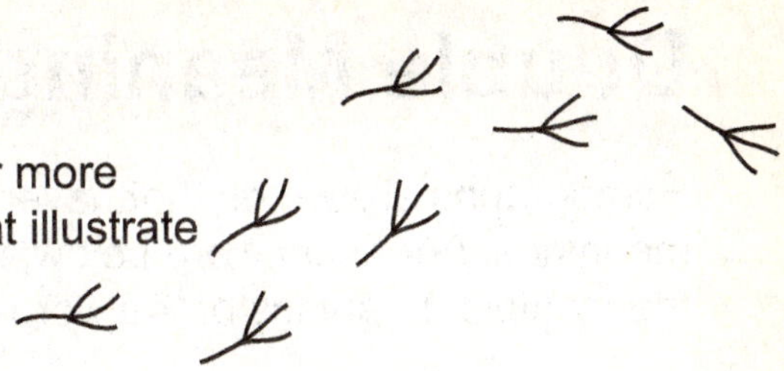

Homographs are words that have one spelling, but two or more meanings. For every word below, write two sentences that illustrate the multiple meanings of the words.

Break

_____

_____

Track

_____

_____

Fire

_____

_____

Shop

_____

_____

Place

_____

_____

Set

_____

_____

Store

_____

_____

Double Meaning Words

Homographs are words that have one spelling, but two or more meanings. For every word below, write two sentences that illustrate the multiple meanings of the words.

Crash

_____

_____

Dance

_____

_____

Stamp

_____

_____

Taste

_____

_____

Talk

_____

_____

Name

_____

_____

Snack

_____

_____

Great job!

is an Education.com writing superstar

FIGURATIVE LANGUAGE

IDIOMS

Idioms are common phrases that have a different meaning from the actual words used. Choose an idiom from the list. On the next two pages, you will draw a picture to illustrate the literal meaning (what the words really mean) and draw a picture to illustrate the figurative meaning (what the idiom means). Then use the idiom in a sentence that shows its meaning.

Example: "Under the weather"

Literal Meaning (real meaning)	Figurative Meaning (idiom)
	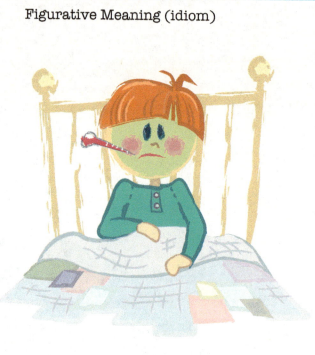

Write in a sentence:

_____

_____

_____

POSSIBLE IDIOMS

A piece of cake	I'm on top of the world	On your high horse
Bite off more than you can chew	I'm in a pickle	Give the cold shoulder
Crack someone up	I'm feeling blue	Talk a mile a minute
Drive someone up the wall	In one ear and out the other	Elbow grease
Hit the nail on the head	That's a piece of cake	Hold down the fort
Back to the drawing board	Give me a hand	Hit the ceiling
Cat got your tongue	Under the weather	Spitting image
Raining cats and dogs	Break a leg	Tie the knot
Wear your heart on your sleeve	You're pulling my leg	Out of the blue
You can't judge a book by its cover	Pass the buck	Pull the plug

Idiom:

Literal Meaning (idiom)	Figurative Meaning (real meaning)

Idiom:

Literal Meaning (idiom)	Figurative Meaning (real meaning)

WRITE A SENTENCE
Choose three idioms from the list on page 22 and use them in sentences below!

Write in a sentence:
_____
_____

Write in a sentence:
_____
_____

Write in a sentence:
_____
_____

IDIOM FILL-INS
Choose the idioms that complete the sentences.

1. Are you guys going to tie the _____ this year?

2. After disappointing sales, the company decided to pull the _____ on the new SUV.

3. This could never happen; are you pulling my _____?

4. I just got a nice promotion at work, now I feel like I'm on top of the _____!

5. After the unsuccessful test, we had to go back to the _____ board.

6. That test was a piece of _____!

7. These hyper dogs are driving me _____!

8. Can you get off your high _____ and give me a _____.

9. With a little bit of elbow _____ we can have this car up and running in no time.

10. It was like I was talking to a wall, in one _____ and out the _____.

Hold the HOMOGRAPHS!!!

Homographs are words that look the same but have more than one meaning, and sometimes more than one pronunciation. For example, there is an animal called a "bat", and there is also a "bat" that baseball players use to hit the ball.

Read the definitions below and write down the homograph that best fits both sentences.

1. The front of a ship OR a ribbon tied up in a girl's hair.

2. A place for stray animals OR 16 ounces.

3. The outer layer of a tree OR the sound a dog makes.

4. A person who rules a country OR something used to measure.

5. A type of flower OR the past tense of "to rise".

6. The earth beneath you OR the past tense of "to grind".

7. A type of tree that grows in warm climates OR a part of your hand.

8. Spectacles you wear to improve vision OR cups to drink from.

9. To rip something OR a fluid that comes from the eye.

10. To be a short distance away OR to cover an opening.

RIDDLE CHALLENGE!

Why was the picture sent to jail?

DOUBLE MEANING

Use each pair of pictures and clues to figure out the homographs!

OR: A PLACE WITH TREES

_____

OR: TO CLING TO SOMETHING

_____

OR: AN ADJECTIVE TO DESCRIBE
SOMEONE SMART

_____

OR: TO HIT SOMETHING WITH
YOUR FISTS

_____

OR: 2 THINGS THAT GO TOGETHER

_____

OR: A LOUD NOISE

_____

PLAYING WITH FIGURATIVE LANGUAGE:
THE METAPHOR GAME

Have you ever heard of a metaphor? Poets make metaphors all the time when they compare things thatare very different from each other. The poet Emily Dickinson wrote a poem comparing hope to a little bird.

You can do this too. It is a fun way to think about the things around you and see them in new ways. Here is a game you can play to help you make your own metaphor and maybe even write a poem.

CREATE YOUR METAPHOR

Cut out the noun word cards on pages 29–37, so that you have nine small pieces of paper. Put these in a container or lay them face down. Close your eyes and choose a noun. In the space provided on the next page, list everything you can think of that the noun does. (For example, for a car you might write things like: It sits in our driveway. It moves forward. It takes us places. It spews exhaust and pollutes the air. It holds my whole family and makes us squeeze together.) Choose a second noun word card. This will be the subject of your metaphor. Write this noun at the top of your list to see how well your metaphor comes together.

LOOK AT YOUR METAPHOR

If you followed the directions carefully you will have created something very interesting that begins with one thing but describes what a totally different thing does. You might think "Wow, I can see how a river does the same things as a pencil!"

If you like what you wrote, you might want to copy it over as a poem. You may want to cross out lines that just seem silly or don't fit in with what you want to say and replace them with other things that you have thought of.

TRY ANOTHER ONE!

If you don't like the first one you wrote, try another. It may take a few tries before you make a metaphor that you like. Also, you can put any words in your container that you want. It's fun to try abstract nouns like hope, joy, and fear.

WRITE IT OUT

Noun #1: _____

Subject of Metaphor: (noun #2)_____
(choose after filling in the blanks below for Noun #1.)

It
_____

It
_____

It also
_____

And sometimes it
_____

But most importantly, it
_____

Noun #1: _____

Subject of Metaphor: (noun #2)_____
(choose after filling in the blanks below for Noun #1.)

It
_____

It
_____

It also
_____

And sometimes it
_____

But most importantly, it
_____

tree

rollercoaster

snake

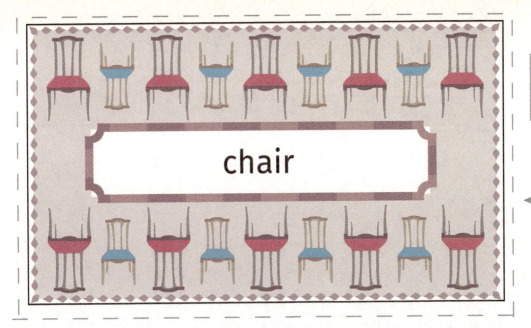

chair

Cut along dotted line

comb

river

shoes

Cut along dotted line

house

pencil

Cut along
dotted line

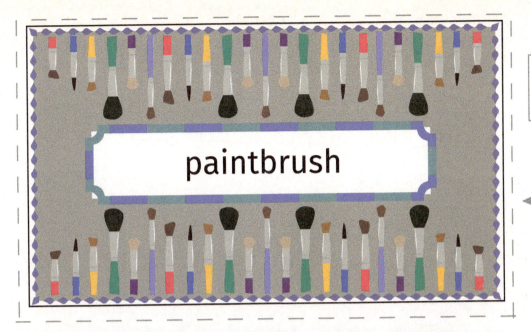

paintbrush

lightning

rocket

elephant

Cut along dotted line

snowflake

cheese

Similes

A simile is a phrase or figure of speech that compares two things using the words "like" or "as".
Compare things in an interesting or unexpected way that creates an image for the reader using "like" or "as" to compare something to a seemingly dissimilar noun, verb, or adjective.
Examples: "She is as strong as an ox," or "he was as quiet as a mouse."

Pattern 1: "like"
verb + like + noun

Examples
She swims like a fish.
He walks like a duck.
She acts like a fool.

Pattern 2: "as"
as + adjective + as + noun

Examples
He is as tall as a giant.
She is as graceful as a swan.
He was as quiet as a mouse.

Fill in the blanks to finish these similes then add more of your own.

1. _____ felt like _____.

2. _____ seems as dark as _____.

3. _____ stopped me like _____.

4. _____ as slimy as _____.

5. _____ as lovely as _____.

6. _____ as bright as _____.

7. _____ ran like _____.

8. _____ smelled rotten like _____.

9. _____ danced like _____.

10. _____ as wiggly as _____.

Mixed Practice:
Similes and Metaphors

Read the sentence and circle the 2 words being compared in each sentence. Determine whether each sentence is a *simile* or a *metaphor*, and write down the meaning based on the context of the sentence.

Example: She (walks) like a (duck.)

         Meaning: Simile – The girl walks funny.

1. Steven sings like a nightingale.

Meaning:

_____

2. The candle is a beacon of sunshine.

Meaning:

_____

3. The moon is a lantern in the sky.

Meaning:

_____

4. Kirsten sleeps like a log.

Meaning:

_____

5. Gretchen is a fish when she swims.

Meaning:

_____

6. Phillip is lightning when he runs a race.

Meaning:

_____

7. The bunny's fur is a blanket of warmth.

Meaning:

_____

8. Anne's voice is velvet.

Meaning:

_____

9. Peter is as sweet as pie.

Meaning:

_____

10. Chris is like a computer when he does his math.

Meaning:

_____

Similes and Metaphors!

Figure out whether each sentence below is a simile or a metaphor. Then, write down the meaning of each metaphor/simile based on how it is being used in a sentence!

Example: You are a couch potato.

Meaning: Metaphor – Someone who sits and does nothing.

1. She eats like a pig!

_____

2. This contract is as solid as the ground we stand on.

_____

3. The world is my oyster.

_____

4. That guy is as nutty as a fruitcake.

_____

5. She is such an airhead.

_____

6. Don't just sit there like a bump on a log.

_____

7. He's a diamond in the rough.

_____

8. Time is a thief.

_____

9. As hard as nails.

_____

10. You are my sunshine.

_____

Draw a Picture!

Using the similes in the box below, pick two, write them down on the line below each box, and draw a picture illustrating what is happening in each.

As brave as a lion
As quick as lightning
As busy as a bee
To drink like a fish
As big as an elephant
To eat like a bird
As cool as a cucumber
As dry as a bone
To sleep like a baby
As clear as a bell
Eyes like a hawk
To smell like a pig
As light as a feather
To fight like a tiger
As poor as dirt
To live like a king
To sing like an angel
To dance like a ballerina
To lie like a snake

OVER THE TOP
Hyperbole

In literature, figurative language refers to the use of images or phrases that make different kinds of comparisons. One type of figurative language is called *hyperbole*, which is an obvious and usually funny exaggeration. For example, you may have heard the phrase, "I am so hungry I could eat a horse!" This is hyperbole, since it is not meant to be serious and is over-the-top to make a point. Good hyperbole is so exaggerated that the reader knows immediately that you are joking.

Complete each sentence using a hyperbole of your own creation!

1. I sat in one place so long during the painting class that _____
_____.

2. The house was as big as a _____.

3. After working out for months I was as strong as an _____.

4. My dog made the funniest noise yesterday. It sounded like _____
_____.

5. After I got straight A's on my report card, I was so happy that I could _____.

PERSONIFICATION

Personification: giving an animal or object human-like characteristics, qualities, or feelings

Read the two passages and underline examples of personification. Explain why the poet used personification to describe the subject of each poem.

The Railway Train
By Emily Dickinson

I like to see it lap the miles,
And lick the valleys up,
And stop to feed itself at tanks;
And then, prodigious, step

Around a pile of mountains,
And, supercilious, peer
In shanties by the sides of roads;
And then a quarry pare

To fit its sides, and crawl between,
Complaining all the while
In horrid, hooting stanza;
Then chase itself down hill

And neigh like Boanerges;
Then, punctual as a star,
Stop — docile and omnipotent —
At its own stable door.

_____
_____
_____
_____
_____

The Moon
by Emily Dickinson

The moon was but a chin of gold
A night or two ago,
And now she turns her perfect face
Upon the world below.

Her forehead is of amplest blond;
Her cheek like beryl stone;
Her eye unto the summer dew
The likest I have known.

Her lips of amber never part;
But what must be the smile
Upon her friend she could bestow
Were such her silver will!

And what a privilege to be
But the remotest star!
For certainly her way might pass
Beside your twinkling door.

Her bonnet is the firmament,
The universe her shoe,
The stars the trinkets at her belt,
Her dimities of blue.

WRITING PROMPT

Now write your own examples of personification! Jot down the characteristics, qualities, and feelings for each subject word, and write a sentence using personification.

1. Ocean
CHARACTERISTICS: _____
QUALITIES: _____
FEELINGS: _____
Write a Sentence: _____

2. Snow
CHARACTERISTICS: _____
QUALITIES: _____
FEELINGS: _____
Write a Sentence: _____

3. River
CHARACTERISTICS: _____
QUALITIES: _____
FEELINGS: _____
Write a Sentence: _____

4. Monkey
CHARACTERISTICS: _____
QUALITIES: _____
FEELINGS: _____
Write a Sentence: _____

5. Pickles
CHARACTERISTICS: _____
QUALITIES: _____
FEELINGS: _____
Write a Sentence: _____
_____

Alliteration

An alliteration repeats consonant sounds at the beginning of words.

Example:

"A Basketful of Berries"

Guys and girls are grabbing great
handfuls of big beautiful blueberries from the bushes.
Bouncing berries in their palms,
some stuff their pockets, picknic baskets, and pails full.
They'll bake blueberry bread,
can jars of jam and jiggling jelly.
Don't delay, it's berry-picking day!

A good way to spot alliteration in a sentence is to sound out the sentence, looking for words with identical consonant sounds. Read through these sentences. Identify and circle the alliteration.

1. Anna ate some awful appetizers.

2. Harry hit Henry on the head.

3. Frank found a pack of furry foxes.

4. Edward eats eggs, enjoying each exquisite bite.

5. Fred's friends fried chicken for Friday's food.

6. Gretchen's giraffe gobbled the tree leaves greedily.

7. Barney bounced back, causing banging and booming.

8. Heather's hamster hungrily awaits his food.

9. Izzie's ice cream is interestingly delicious.

10. Jackson's jackrabbit is jumping and jiggling all over the place.

ASSONANCE -AND- CONSONANCE

ASSONANCE is the repetition of vowel sounds in words that are close together. It's the sound that is important and not the letters used.
Examples: *"By twinkling twilight he sang a nice song to pass the night"* (Long i)
"Two tulips danced to music on the wind" (Long u)

Don't confuse assonance with alliteration. The "tw" in twinkling and twlight are alliteration because these consonant sounds are at the beginning of the words. The "t" sound in two, tulips and to is also alliteration.

CONSONANCE is the repetition of consonant sounds at the ends of words and that follow stressed syllables in words close together.
Examples: *"Norm, the worm, weathered the storm without harm."*
"Errors occurred when the editor of the story slept."

Read the poem below and circle each case of assonance or consonance.
Hint: Read the poem out loud so you can really hear the sound of the words.

THE RAVEN
By Edgar Allan Poe

Once upon a midnight dreary, while I pondered weak and weary,

Over many a quaint and curious volume of forgotten lore—

While I nodded, nearly napping, suddenly there came a tapping,

As of someone gently rapping, rapping at my chamber door.

"'Tis some visitor," I muttered, "tapping at my chamber door;

Only this and nothing more."

Assonance and consonance are often used together. Read the quotes below and figure out where assonance and/or consonance are being used. Then write down what sounds are being repeated.

EXAMPLE: O̲r hear old Triton blow his wreathed h**o**rn.   _o-Assonance_

1. From the molten golden notes, _____

2. Her finger hungered for a ring. _____

3. Cupid laid by his brand. _____

4. How they clang, and clash, _____

5. and roar! What a horror they outpour. _____

6. Whose woods these are I think I know. _____

7. He saw the cost and hauled off. _____

8. Gayle tapped a finger on the sack of books in her lap.

_____

9. I sipped the rim with palatable lip. _____

10. A gallant knight, in sunshine and in shadow, _____

11. "Thou art a fool," said my head to my heart. _____

12. What a world of merriment their melody foretells!

_____

13. It was half as funny after, when they laughed so at the staff.

_____

14. Well that was short but sweet. _____

ONOMATOPOEIA

An **onomatopoeia** (pronounced: on-oh-mat-oh-PEA-uh) is a word that imitates the sound that it describes.

Choose a word from the word bank to help complete the sentences.

quack
pop
tick
roar
bark
snap
chatter
swish
crackle
bang
screech
sizzle
click
chirp
buzz

1. The bird loved to _____ a merry tune.

2. The _____ of the clock kept me up all night.

3. The food on the stove made a nice _____.

4. She kept making a _____ noise with her pen and it drove the teacher crazy!

5. The little dogs like to _____ at the cat.

6. Something upset the lion and it made a loud _____.

7. I heard the ruler _____ against the desk.

8. His teeth started to _____ outside in the cold.

9. The fire made a _____ when they added more wood.

10. As the car started up it made a loud _____.

11. The chalk _____ on the black board.

12. The wheel went _____ as we ran over a nail in the road.

13. The ducklings _____ behind their mother.

14. Her dress makes a _____ noise as she walks.

15. The bees happily _____ around the garden.

Great job!

_____

is an Education.com writing superstar

PETER PAN AND NEVERLAND

To Grow Up or *Not to Grow Up?*

The story of Peter Pan begins as follows:

All children, except one, grow up. They soon know that they will grow up, and the way Wendy knew was this. One day when she was two years old she was playing in a garden, and she plucked another flower and ran with it to her mother. I suppose she must have looked rather delightful, for Mrs. Darling put her hand to her heart and cried, "Oh, why can't you remain like this forever!" This was all that passed between them on the subject, but henceforth Wendy knew that she must grow up. You always know after you are two. Two is the beginning of the end.

This passage suggests that there is some sadness associated with remaining a child forever. What are the pros and cons?

Pros	Cons

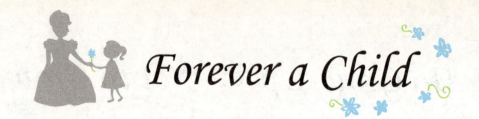

Forever a Child

Would it be good or bad to stay a child forever?

Use your ideas to write a persuasive paragraph that includes your opinion,
supported by at least three strong points.

Visualizing Neverland

In the story of Peter Pan, the main characters take a magical flight to Neverland. Neverland is described in the following passage:

I don't know whether you have ever seen a map of a person's mind. Doctors sometimes draw maps of other parts of you, and your own map can become intensely interesting, but catch them trying to draw a map of a child's mind, which is not only confused, but keeps going round all the time. There are zigzag lines on it, just like your temperature on a card, and these are probably roads in the island, for the Neverland is always more or less an island, with astonishing splashes of colour here and there, and coral reefs and rakish-looking craft in the offing, and savages and lonely lairs, and gnomes who are mostly tailors, and caves through which a river runs, and princes with six elder brothers, and a hut fast going into decay, and one very small old lady with a hooked nose. It would be an easy map if that were all, but there is also first day at school, religion, fathers, the round pond, needle-work...chocolate pudding day, getting into braces, say ninety-nine, three-pence for pulling out your tooth yourself, and so on, and either these are part of the island or they are another map showing through, and it is all rather confusing, especially as nothing will stand still.

Neverland exists in the mind of each child. Draw your interpretation of Neverland using details from the passage above, along with your own ideas.

Read the passage below from J.M. Barrie's *Peter Pan*
then complete the worksheets that follow.

Chapter 4: The Flight

∿ Part 1 ∿

"Second to the right, and straight on till morning."

That, Peter had told Wendy, was the way to the Neverland; but even birds, carrying maps and consulting them at windy corners, could not have sighted it with these instructions. Peter, you see, just said anything that came into his head.

At first his companions trusted him implicitly, and so great were the delights of flying that they wasted time circling round church spires or any other tall objects on the way that took their fancy.

John and Michael raced, Michael getting a start.

They recalled with contempt that not so long ago they had thought themselves fine fellows for being able to fly round a room.

Not so long ago. But how long ago? They were flying over the sea before this thought began to disturb Wendy seriously. John thought it was their second sea and their third night.

Sometimes it was dark and sometimes light, and now they were very cold and again too warm. Did they really feel hungry at times, or were they merely pretending, because Peter had such a jolly new way of feeding them? His way was to pursue birds who had food in their mouths suitable for humans and snatch it from them;

then the birds would follow and snatch it back; and they would all go chasing each other gaily for miles, parting at last with mutual expressions of good-will. But Wendy noticed with gentle concern that Peter did not seem to know that this was rather an odd way of getting your bread and butter, nor even that there are other ways.

Certainly they did not pretend to be sleepy, they were sleepy; and that was a danger, for the moment they popped off, down they fell. The awful thing was that Peter thought this funny.

"There he goes again!" he would cry gleefully, as Michael suddenly dropped like a stone.

"Save him, save him!" cried Wendy, looking with horror at the cruel sea far below. Eventually Peter would dive through the air, and catch Michael just before he could strike the sea, and it was lovely the way he did it; but he always waited till the last moment, and you felt it was his cleverness that interested him more. Also he was fond of variety, and the sport that engrossed him one moment would suddenly cease to engage him, so there was always the possibility that the next time you fell he would let you go.

He could sleep in the air without falling, by merely lying on his back and floating, but this was, partly at least, because he was so light that if you got behind him and blew he went faster.

58

Vocabulary Practice

Answer the vocabulary questions below and refer back to the text as needed.

~ *Part 1* ~

Definitions

Write the letter in the blank space next to the correct definition.

a. consulting   _____ to take up all of your attention

b. implicitly   _____ sharing the same feeling

c. contempt   _____ without question

d. disturb   _____ bother or trouble

e. mutual   _____ to check for advice or information

f. engrossed   _____ to have negative feelings towards something or someone

Find a word in the text that means:

happy _____   scared _____

tired _____   bad _____

59

Peter Pan
J.M.Barrie

Read the passage below from J.M. Barrie's *Peter Pan*
then complete the worksheets that follow.

Chapter 4: The Flight

~ Part 2 ~

"Do be more polite to him," Wendy whispered to John, when they were playing "Follow the Leader."

"Then tell him to stop showing off," said John.

When playing Follow the Leader, Peter would fly close to the water and touch each shark's tail in passing, just as in the street you may run your finger along an iron railing. They could not follow him in this with much success, so perhaps it was rather like showing off, especially as he kept looking behind to see how many tails they missed.

"You must be nice to him," Wendy impressed on her brothers. "What could we do if he were to leave us?"

"We could go back," Michael said.

"How could we ever find our way back home without him?"

"Well, then, we could go on," said John.

"That is the awful thing, John. We should have to go on, for we don't know how to stop."

This was true; Peter had forgotten to show them how to stop.

John said that if the worst came to the worst, all they had to do was to go straight on, for the world was round, and so in time they must come back to their own window.

"And who is to get food for us, John?"

"I nipped a bit out of that eagle's mouth pretty neatly, Wendy."

"After the twentieth try," Wendy reminded him. "And even though we became good at picking up food, see how we bump against clouds and things if he is not near to give us a hand."

Indeed they were constantly bumping. They could now fly strongly, though they still kicked far too much; but if they saw a cloud in front of them, the more they tried to avoid it, the more certainly did they bump into it. If Nana had been with them, she would have had a bandage round Michael's forehead by this time.

Peter was not with them for the moment, and they felt rather lonely up there by themselves. He could go so much faster than they that he would suddenly shoot out of sight, to have some adventure in which they had no share. He would come down laughing over something fearfully funny he had been saying to a star, but he had already forgotten what it was, or he would come up with mermaid scales still sticking to him, and yet not be able to say for certain what had been happening. It was really rather irritating to children who had never seen a mermaid.

Reading Comprehension

Based on the reading from Chapter 4 of *Peter Pan,* answer the questions below about Wendy's character.

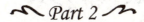 *Part 2*

How would you describe Wendy? (circle one or more)

kind   nurturing   sad   bossy   serious   outgoing   other _____

Why? Use evidence from the text to support your ideas.

What Wendy says: _____

_____

_____

What Wendy does: _____

_____

_____

What other characters say or think about her: _____

_____

_____

_____

Do you think Wendy would be a good sister to have? Why?: _____

_____

_____

Vocabulary Practice

Peter Pan
J.M.Barrie

Answer the vocabulary questions below and refer back to the text as needed.

Part 2

Definitions

Write the letter in the blank space next to the correct definition.

a. polite

b. impressed

c. reminded

d. constantly

e. scales

f. irritating

_____ to help someone remember

_____ thin, overlapping plates

_____ to emphasize or urge something

_____ to be annoying

_____ something happening over and over

_____ showing good manners towards others

What do you think?

In your own words, write definitions for the following:

• fearfully _____

_____

• mermaid _____

_____

62

Read the passage below from J.M. Barrie's *Peter Pan*
then complete the worksheets that follow.

Chapter 4: The Flight

∼ Part 3 ∼

"And if he forgets them, so quickly," Wendy argued, "how can we expect that he will go on remembering us?"

Indeed, sometimes when he returned he did not remember them, at least not well. Wendy was sure of it. She saw recognition come into his eyes as he was about to pass them the time of day and go on; once even she had to tell him her name.

"I'm Wendy," she said agitatedly.

He was very sorry. "I say, Wendy," he whispered to her, "always if you see me forgetting you, just keep on saying 'I'm Wendy,' and then I'll remember."

Of course this was rather unsatisfactory. However, to make amends he showed them how to lie out flat on a strong wind that was going their way, and this was such a pleasant change that they tried it several times and found they could sleep thus with security. Indeed they would have slept longer, but Peter tired quickly of sleeping, and soon he would cry in his captain voice, "We get off here."

So with occasional tiffs, but on the whole rollicking, they drew near the Neverland; for after many moons they did reach it, and, what is more, they had been going pretty straight all the time, not perhaps so much owing to the guidance of Peter or Tink as because the island was out looking for them. It is only thus that any one may sight those magic shores.

"There it is," said Peter calmly.

"Where, where?"

"Where all the arrows are pointing."

Indeed a million golden arrows were pointing out the island to the children, all directed by their friend the sun, who wanted them to be sure of their way before leaving them for the night.

Vocabulary Practice

Peter Pan
J.M.Barrie

Answer the vocabulary questions below and refer back to the text as needed.

~ *Part 3* ~

Definitions

Write the letter in the blank space next to the correct definition.

a. recognition   _____ knowing someone

b. agitatedly   _____ not good enough

c. unsatisfactory   _____ sometimes

d. amends   _____ upset or disturbed

e. occasional   _____ carefree or with high spirits

f. rollicking   _____ to make up for

Antonyms

Antonyms are words that have the opposite meaning of another word. For example, WET and DRY.
Find the antonym in the text for the following words:

enemy _____   laugh _____

weak _____   yelled _____

far _____   crooked _____

Reading Comprehension

What does Neverland represent for Peter? For Wendy?

Peter	Wendy

Peter Pan:
YOUR Tour Guide to Neverland?

In Chapter 4, Peter Pan shows himself to be a very dynamic character and leader for the children. Which leadershp qualities does he have? Which does he lack?

Qualities Peter Has	Qualities Peter Lacks

Explain whether you would follow him to Neverland or not. Support your opinion with evidence from the text.

_____

_____

_____

_____

_____

_____

_____

_____

Meet Peter Pan:
Using Context Clues to Understand a Character

Reread the passages from Chapter 4 carefully. Write what each reveals about Peter Pan.

"Save him, save him!" cried Wendy, looking with horror at the cruel sea far below. Eventually Peter would dive through the air, and catch Michael just before he could strike the sea, and it was lovely the way he did it; but he always waited till the last moment, and you felt it was his cleverness that interested him and not the saving of human life. Also he was fond of variety, and the sport that engrossed him one moment would suddenly cease to engage him, so there was always the possibility that the next time you fell he would let you go.

_____

_____

_____

_____

Indeed, sometimes when he returned he did not remember them, at least not well. Wendy was sure of it. She saw recognition come into his eyes as he was about to pass them the time of day and go on; once even she had to call him by name.
"I'm Wendy," she said agitatedly.
He was very sorry. "I say, Wendy," he whispered to her, "always if you see me forgetting you, just keep on saying 'I'm Wendy,' and then I'll remember."

_____

_____

_____

_____

They had been flying apart, but they huddled close to Peter now. His careless manner had gone at last, his eyes were sparkling, and a tingle went through them every time they touched his body. They were now over the fearsome island, flying so low that sometimes a tree grazed their feet. Nothing horrid was visible in the air, yet their progress had become slow and laboured, exactly as if they were pushing their way through hostile forces. Sometimes they hung in the air until Peter had beaten on it with his fists.

_____

_____

_____

_____

Think Outside the Box:
Tidying Your Mind!

The following passage from Peter Pan describes a mother's nightly ritual of cleaning up and organizing her children's minds while they sleep:

Mrs. Darling first heard of Peter when she was tidying up her children's minds. It is the nightly custom of every good mother after her children are asleep to rummage in their minds and put things straight for next morning, repacking into their proper places the many articles that have wandered during the day. If you could keep awake (but of course you can't) you would see your own mother doing this, and you would find it very interesting to watch her. It is quite like tidying up drawers. You would see her on her knees, I expect, lingering humorously over some of your contents, wondering where on earth you had picked this thing up, making discoveries sweet and not so sweet, pressing this to her cheek as if it were as nice as a kitten, and hurriedly stowing that out of sight. When you wake in the morning, the naughtiness and evil passions with which you went to bed have been folded up small and placed at the bottom of your mind and on the top, beautifully aired, are spread out your prettier thoughts, ready for you to put on.

Just for fun, show YOUR mind before you go to sleep and what it would look like after your parents come and clean it up.

Before	After

You Tell the Story

J.M. Barrie draws a vivid picture of the character Peter Pan, but still leaves much to the reader's imagination. Read the passage below and add your own ideas to the scene!

Peter was not with them for the moment, and they felt rather lonely up there by themselves. He could go so much faster than they that he would suddenly shoot out of sight, to have some adventure in which they had no share. He would come down laughing over something fearfully funny he had been saying to a star, but he had already forgotten what it was, or he would come up with mermaid scales still sticking to him, and yet not be able to say for certain what had been happening. It was really rather irritating to children who had never seen a mermaid.

What funny thing does Peter Pan say to the star?

What explains the mermaid scales?

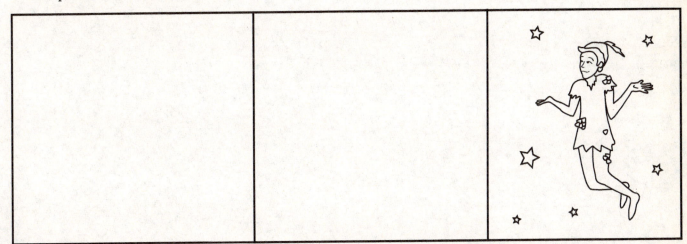

Make your Mark!

Jot down character notes about Peter and Wendy on the back of these bookmarks or get creative and draw your own.
Find a copy of *Peter Pan* and keep track of where you left off with these fun bookmarks!

Peter Pan

Wendy

Great job!

is an Education.com reading superstar

BOOK MARKS
THE SPOT

Navigate This Workbook

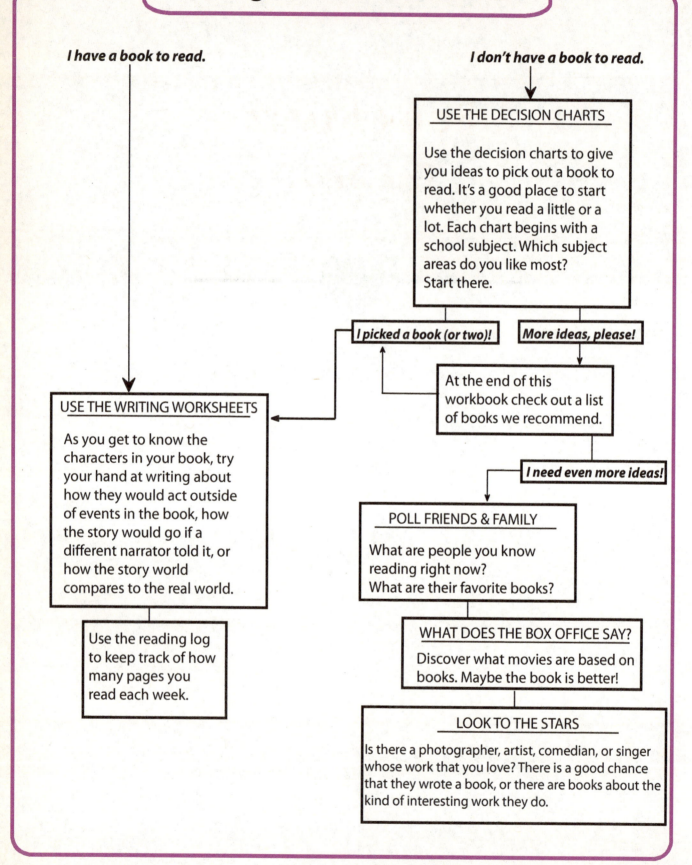

I have a book to read.

I don't have a book to read.

USE THE DECISION CHARTS

Use the decision charts to give you ideas to pick out a book to read. It's a good place to start whether you read a little or a lot. Each chart begins with a school subject. Which subject areas do you like most? Start there.

I picked a book (or two)!

More ideas, please!

At the end of this workbook check out a list of books we recommend.

I need even more ideas!

USE THE WRITING WORKSHEETS

As you get to know the characters in your book, try your hand at writing about how they would act outside of events in the book, how the story would go if a different narrator told it, or how the story world compares to the real world.

Use the reading log to keep track of how many pages you read each week.

POLL FRIENDS & FAMILY

What are people you know reading right now?
What are their favorite books?

WHAT DOES THE BOX OFFICE SAY?

Discover what movies are based on books. Maybe the book is better!

LOOK TO THE STARS

Is there a photographer, artist, comedian, or singer whose work that you love? There is a good chance that they wrote a book, or there are books about the kind of interesting work they do.

Fact File

Fill in the following information about your chosen book.

Title: _____

Author: _____

Number of Pages: _____

Genre: _____

Main Characters:

_____

_____

_____

_____

Plot: _____

_____

_____

_____

_____

_____

Language Arts

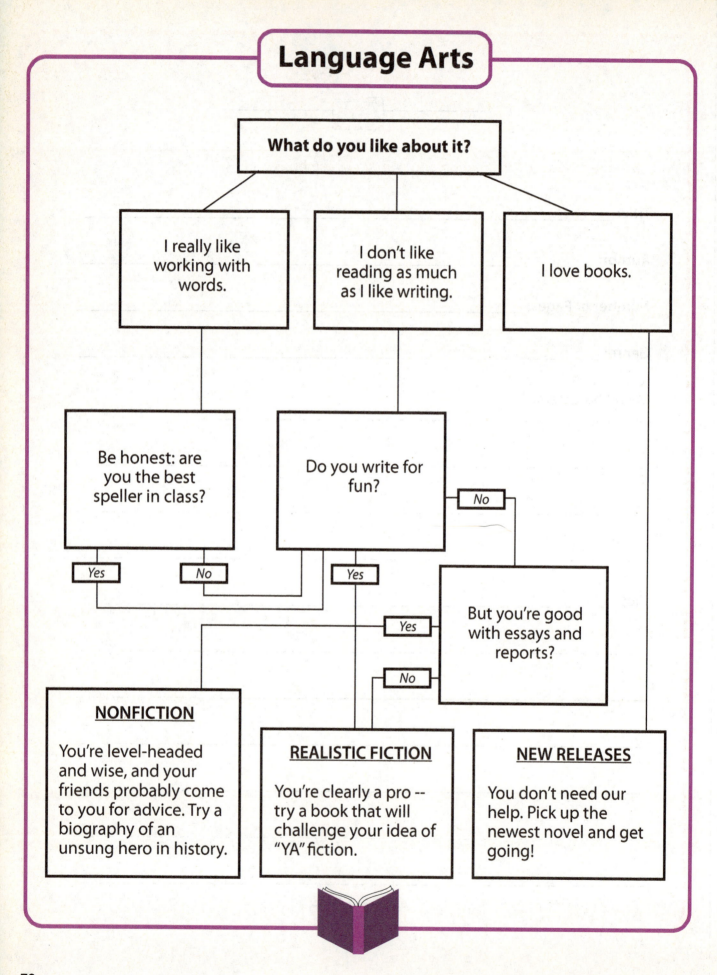

What do you like about it?

I really like working with words.

I don't like reading as much as I like writing.

I love books.

Be honest: are you the best speller in class?

Do you write for fun?

No

Yes

No

Yes

Yes

No

But you're good with essays and reports?

NONFICTION

You're level-headed and wise, and your friends probably come to you for advice. Try a biography of an unsung hero in history.

REALISTIC FICTION

You're clearly a pro -- try a book that will challenge your idea of "YA" fiction.

NEW RELEASES

You don't need our help. Pick up the newest novel and get going!

Math and Science

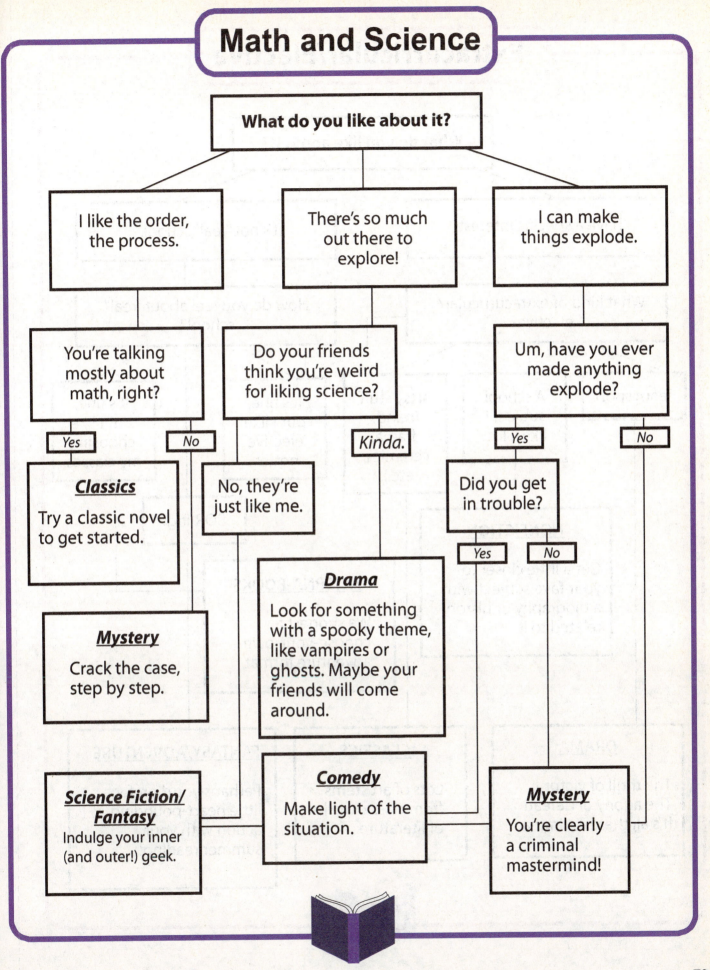

What do you like about it?

- I like the order, the process.
- There's so much out there to explore!
- I can make things explode.

I like the order, the process. → You're talking mostly about math, right?
- **Yes** → **_Classics_** Try a classic novel to get started.
- **No** → **_Mystery_** Crack the case, step by step.

There's so much out there to explore! → Do your friends think you're weird for liking science?
- No, they're just like me. → **_Science Fiction/Fantasy_** Indulge your inner (and outer!) geek.
- **Kinda.** → **_Drama_** Look for something with a spooky theme, like vampires or ghosts. Maybe your friends will come around.

I can make things explode. → Um, have you ever made anything explode?
- **Yes** → Did you get in trouble?
  - **Yes** → **_Comedy_** Make light of the situation.
  - **No** → **_Mystery_** You're clearly a criminal mastermind!
- **No** → **_Mystery_** You're clearly a criminal mastermind!

Extracurricular/Elective

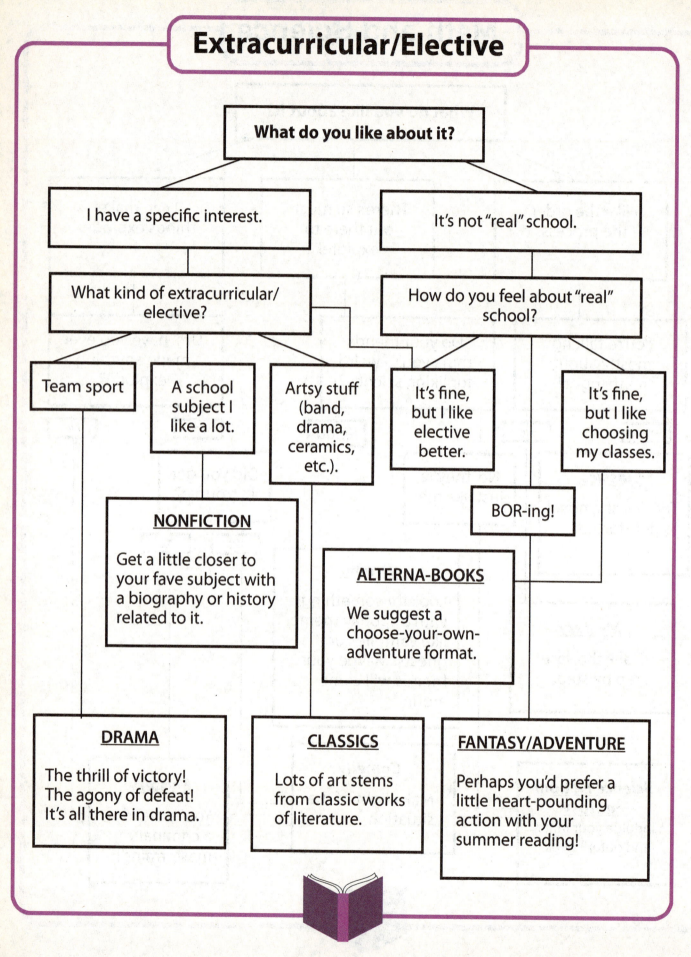

What do you like about it?

I have a specific interest.

It's not "real" school.

What kind of extracurricular/ elective?

How do you feel about "real" school?

Team sport

A school subject I like a lot.

Artsy stuff (band, drama, ceramics, etc.).

It's fine, but I like elective better.

It's fine, but I like choosing my classes.

BOR-ing!

NONFICTION

Get a little closer to your fave subject with a biography or history related to it.

ALTERNA-BOOKS

We suggest a choose-your-own-adventure format.

DRAMA

The thrill of victory! The agony of defeat! It's all there in drama.

CLASSICS

Lots of art stems from classic works of literature.

FANTASY/ADVENTURE

Perhaps you'd prefer a little heart-pounding action with your summer reading!

Casting Call!

Pretend you're making a movie or play of the book and you need to cast actors for it. What should the actors look like? What kind of personalities will they need to portray? Write character descriptions and cast famous actors on the lines below.

Main Character: _____

Description: _____

_____

_____

Actor: _____

Main Character: _____

Description: _____

_____

_____

Actor: _____

Supporting Character: _____

Description: _____

_____

_____

Actor: _____

Supporting Character: _____

Description: _____

_____

_____

Actor: _____

Script

Using the character descriptions you just wrote, turn a chapter of your book into a script.

Main Character 1: _____

_____

Main Character 2: _____

_____

Supporting Character: _____

_____

Main Character 1: _____

_____

Main Character 2: _____

_____

Supporting Character: _____

_____

Main Character 1: _____

_____

Fan Fiction

Fan fiction is fiction written by fans like you! It takes characters from a book or series and puts them in new stories created by fans. Have an idea for an alternate ending to your book? Think you know what happens to the characters after the book ends? Write your own fan fiction on the lines below!

_____

_____

_____

_____

_____

_____

_____

_____

_____

_____

_____

Fiction to Fact

Read a newspaper, watch a TV news program, or listen to a radio news broadcast. Select a current event that relates to the events in your book. How are the events the same? How are they different? Write a paragraph comparing the two.

_____

_____

_____

_____

_____

_____

_____

_____

_____

_____

_____

_____

_____

Poster

Create a poster for the movie or play version of your book. Don't forget to include a *tagline*, the text at the bottom of the poster that makes people want to go see the show!

Book Character Quiz

Turn regular reading comprehension on its head with this writing activity -- a book character quiz!

What You Need:

•   Fiction novel previously read and enjoyed
•   Paper, pen, pencil
•   Character Traits chart

What You Do:

1. Pick a fictional book you like that has at least three distinct main characters.

2. Fill out a Character Traits chart like the one on the next page for three main characters from your book.

3. After you've filled out the chart, work on a "Which Character Do You Resemble?" quiz. Write a multiple-choice question that quizzes someone about their personality based on one item from the chart. For example, for this chart, a question could be:

   When you get on a stage, you tend to:
   a. shine like a star and talk freely.
   b. shy away from the spotlight.
   c. sing a song.

   If you were to give this question to a friend, you would know that a friend answering "a" resembles the character Peeta.

4. Repeat step #3 to write more quiz questions. Make sure to write a variety of questions so that a quiz-taker could get answers resembling each one of the three characters.

5. After you're done writing questions, write the scoring system. This will tell the player what an answer means for each question.

6. Give the quiz to friends to find out which book character they most resemble!

Book Character Quiz

Traits:	Character's name: Katniss Everdeen	Character's name: Peeta Mellark	Character's name: Haymitch Abernathy
Things Character Says:	"I volunteer!" Kind people have a way of working their way inside me and rooting there.	"She has no idea. The effect she can have." "Remember, we're madly in love, so it's all right to kiss me anytime you feel like it."	"Did I actually get a pair of fighters this year?" "sweetheart"
Things Character Does:	Hunts illegally. Volunteers for her sister. Takes care of her family. Gets shy, uncomfortable or uncooperative in public spotlight.	Protects Katniss, to make sure she gets out of the Games alive. Charms the Capitol people/public.	Drinks a lot. Acts like he doesn't care. Coaches Peeta & Katniss. Helps Katniss with sponsorships during the Games.
Things Character Thinks:	Of how she'll kill tributes to win the Games. Thinks of Prim a lot. Tries to avoid thinking of Gale, and Peeta.	Katniss cares about him, too. How to preserve himself against what the Capitol wants them to be.	Strategy. What to say, how to be, advice for the arena. He's always thinking ahead for the tributes.
Things Character Wears:	Fire dress. Normally she wears a simple shirt and pants and boots.	His clothing is only really mentioned around the Games. He wears a fire outfit too. At one point, a tuxedo.	Not sure actually, this is never really described, except as vomit when he gets sick on himself.
Other General Character Traits:	Short sighted thinking, sometimes disconnected. Good with a bow. Tough. But also sensitive, defensive.	He's smart and generally kind. He's a baker and froster. He's strong. Has a sense of humor.	He won a Hunger Games before. Has had to mentor all Dist. 12 tributes by himself ever since.

Book Character Quiz

Traits:	Character's name: _____	Character's name: _____	Character's name: _____
Things Character Says:			
Things Character Does:			
Things Character Thinks:			
Things Character Wears:			
Other General Character Traits:			

The Main Event!

Write a one-sentence summary of each of the most important events in the book. Then, draw a picture of the event in the box below your summary.

Event #1:

_____

_____

Event #2:

_____

_____

Event #3:

_____

_____

Event #4:

_____

_____

Reading Log

Keep track of your reading progress using the grid below. Each week, fill in the number of pages you read.

Week 1	Number of pages read: _____
Week 2	Number of pages read: _____
Week 3	Number of pages read: _____
Week 4	Number of pages read: _____
Week 5	Number of pages read: _____
Week 6	Number of pages read: _____
Week 7	Number of pages read: _____
Week 8	Number of pages read: _____

Travel Brochure

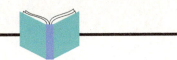

Create a travel brochure for the setting of your book! If the action takes place in multiple locations, use the main location for your travel brochure. Fill in the lines below with a description of the place. What's unique about it? What is it about the place that makes it worth visiting? Draw pictures of the location in the boxes.

Sights to See:

Things to Do:

Travel to:

How to Get There:

Slam Book

Have you ever made a **slam book**? It can be a great way for friends to get to know each other...or it can lead to major hurt feelings! Here's how it works: A name is written at the top of the page of a notebook. The book is passed around to friends or schoolmates, who each write a word or phrase about the person named. It's usually *anonymous*, which means nobody signs their name to what they write.

What would happen if the characters in your book made a slam book? Would they be fair to one another? Would they write kind things or mean things? Choose two characters from your book. If you're reading a biography or a history, choose two of the historical figures you've read about. Write their names at the tops of the notebook pages below. Then, write about each character from the point of view of the other.

Name: _____	Name: _____

Book List

ALTERNA-BOOKS: *Not your average novel!*

<u>Gifts From The Gods</u> by Lise Lunge-Larsen
<u>Best Shorts: Favorite Short Stories for Sharing</u> by Avi
<u>Adventures of Beanboy</u> by Lisa Harkrader
<u>Looking For Me</u> by Betsy R. Rosenthal
<u>Mal and Chad</u> by Stephen McCranie

CLASSICS: *Not old, just vintage.*

<u>The Wind in the Willows</u> by Kenneth Grahame
<u>The Wonderful Wizard of Oz</u> by L. Frank Baum
<u>A Wrinkle in Time</u> by Madeleine L'Engle
<u>Island of the Blue Dolphins</u> by Scott O'Dell

COMEDY: *Laugh your ISBN off!*

<u>Holes</u> by Louis Sachar
<u>The Fizze Whiz Kid</u> by Maiya Williams
<u>The Templeton Twins Have an Idea: Book One</u> by Ellis Weiner

DRAMA: *Grab the tissues.*

<u>Is It Night or Day</u> by Fern Schumer Chapman
<u>A Drowned Maiden's Hair</u> by Laura Amy Schlitz
<u>King Matt the First</u> by Janusz Korczak

FANTASY AND ADVENTURE: *And away we go!*

<u>The Black Book of Secrets</u> by F.E. Higgins
<u>The Silver Bowl</u> by Diane Stanley
<u>The Cabinet of Wonders</u> by Marie Rutkoski
<u>Castle of Shadows</u> by Ellen Renner

Book List

MYSTERY: *Elementary, my dear Watson.*

<u>39 Clues: The Maze of Bones</u> by Rick Riordan
<u>The Secret of Zoom</u> by Lynne Jonell
<u>Tom's Midnight Garden</u> by Philippa Pearce
<u>The Name of This Book is Secret</u> by Pseudonymous Bosch

NONFICTION: *Stranger than fiction.*

<u>Seymour Simon's Extreme Earth Records</u> by Seymour Simon
<u>The Worst Case Scenario Ultimate Adventure: Everest</u> by David
      Borgenicht and Bill Doyle
<u>Kaffir Boy: The True Story of a Black Youth's Coming of Age in Apartheid</u>
      <u>South Africa</u> by Mark Mathabane
<u>Genius: Great Inventors and Their Creations</u> by Jack Challoner

REALISTIC & HISTORICAL FICTION: *Get real.*

<u>The Berlin Boxing Club</u> by Robert Sharenow
<u>Mamba Point</u> by Kurtis Scaletta
<u>Dogtag Summer</u> by Elizabeth Partridge
<u>Maniac Magee</u> by Jerry Spinelli

SCIENCE FICTION: *Take me to your leader.*

<u>Raiders' Ransom</u> by Emily Diamand
<u>The Blackhope Enigma</u> by Teresa Flavin
<u>Fever Crumb</u> by Philip Reeve
<u>The Quartet Series</u> by Lois Lowry

Great job!

is an Education.com reading superstar

ANSWERS

Double Meaning Words

Here are some possible definitions to assist you with your task.

Break

(verb) To make something stop functioning, or change in a detrimental way

(noun) A respite

Track

(verb) To follow

(noun) A pathway

Fire

(noun) A burning mass of material

(verb) To remove someone from their employment

Shop

(verb) To make purchases

(noun) A store

Place

(verb) To put something in particular position

(noun) A specific location

Set

(noun) A collection

(verb) To place something in a particular position

Store

(verb) To put away somewhere

(noun) A place of business

Double Meaning Words

Here are some of the possible definitions to assist you in your task.

Crash

(verb) To break with noise

(noun) A collision

Dance

(verb) To move a body rhythmically

(noun) A group of rhythmical movements organized to music

Stamp

(noun) An adhesive label of postage

(verb) To bring down forcibly

Taste

(verb) To perceive the flavor of by placing on one's tongue

(noun) The sense by which flavor is perceived

Talk

(verb) To communicate verbally

(noun) A lecture

Name

(verb) The act of labelling someone or something

(noun) A word, or words, by which a person is known

Snack

(noun) A small meal between regular meals

(verb) To eat a small meal

Hold the HOMOGRAPHS!!!

Homographs are words that look the same but have more than one meaning, and sometimes more than one pronunciation. For example, there is an animal called a "bat", and there is also a "bat" that baseball players use to hit the ball.

Read the definitions below and write down the homograph that best fits both sentences.

1. The front of a ship OR a ribbon tied up in a girl's hair. bow

2. A place for stray animals OR 16 ounces. pound

3. The outer layer of a tree OR the sound a dog makes. bark

4. A person who rules a country OR something used to measure. ruler

5. A type of flower OR the past tense of "to rise". rose

6. The earth beneath you OR the past tense of "to grind". ground

7. A type of tree that grows in warm climates OR a part of you hand. palm

8. Spectacles you wear to improve vision OR cups to drink from. glasses

9. To rip something OR a fluid that comes from the eye. tear

10. To be a short distance away OR to cover an opening. close

RIDDLE CHALLENGE!

Why wras the picture sent to jail?

Because it was framed.

DOUBLE MEANING

Use each pair of pictures and clues to figure out the homographs!

TO CLING TO SOMETHING
stick

TO HIT SOMETHING WITH YOUR FISTS
punch

A LOUD NOISE
pop

A PLACE WITH TREES
park

AN ADJECTIVE TO DESCRIBE SOMEONE SMART
bright

2 THINGS THAT GO TOGETHER
match

Mixed Practice:
Similes and Metaphors

Read the sentence and circle the 2 words being compared in each sentence. Determine whether each sentence is a *simile* or a *metaphor*, and write down the meaning based on the context of the sentence.

Example: She (walks) like a (duck).

Meaning: Simile – The girl walks funny.

1. Steven sings like a nightingale.

Meaning: Simile – Steven sings beautifully.

2. The candle is a beacon of sunshine.

Meaning: Metaphor – The candle's light in the dark gives me hope, or is very comforting.

3. The moon is a lantern in the sky.

Meaning: Metaphor – The moon shines light.

4. Kirsten sleeps like a log.

Meaning: Simile – Kirsten sleeps very heavily/soundly.

5. Gretchen is a fish when she swims.

Meaning: Metaphor – Gretchen is a good swimmer.

6. Phillip is lightning when he runs a race.

Meaning: Metaphor – Phillip is very fast.

7. The bunny's fur is a blanket of warmth.

Meaning: Metaphor – The bunny's fur is warm.

8. Anne's voice is velvet.

Meaning: Metaphor – Anne has a soft, soothing voice.

9. Peter is as sweet as pie.

Meaning: Simile – Peter is very nice/friendly.

10. Chris is like a computer when he does his math.

Meaning: Simile – Chris is really good at math.

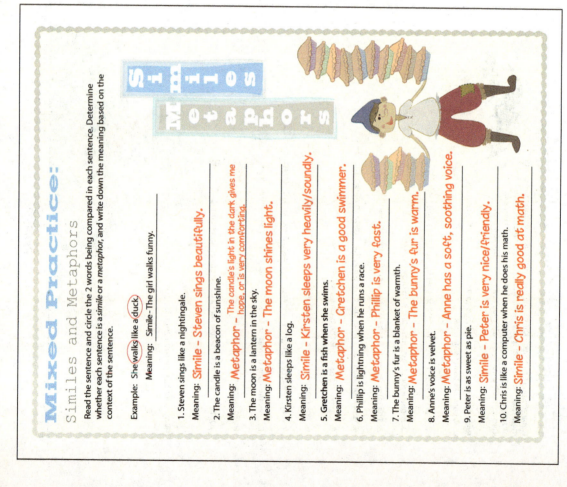

page 40

Similes and Metaphors!

Figure out whether each sentence below is a simile or a metaphor. Then write down the meaning of each sentence below based on how it is being used in a sentence!

Example: You are a couch potato.

Meaning: Metaphor – Someone who sits and does nothing.

1. She eats like a pig!

Simile – She is a messy eater.

2. This contract is as solid as the ground we stand on.

Simile – The contract cannot be broken.

3. The world is my oyster.   The world is mine, and I'm free to do anything! OR

Metaphor –   I get wealth and/or riches from the world.

4. That guy is as nutty as a fruitcake.

Simile – This guy is crazy.

5. She is such an airhead.

Metaphor – She is flakey, unreliable and/or ditzy.

6. Don't just sit there like a bump on a log.

Simile – Don't be lazy and unproductive.

7. He's a diamond in the rough.

Metaphor – He is a rare find.

8. Time is a thief.   Time is a force we can't control,

Metaphor – and it "robs" us of our youth/health.

9. I am as tired as a dog.

Simile – I'm really really tired.

10. You are my sunshine.

Metaphor – I really like you and enjoy your company.

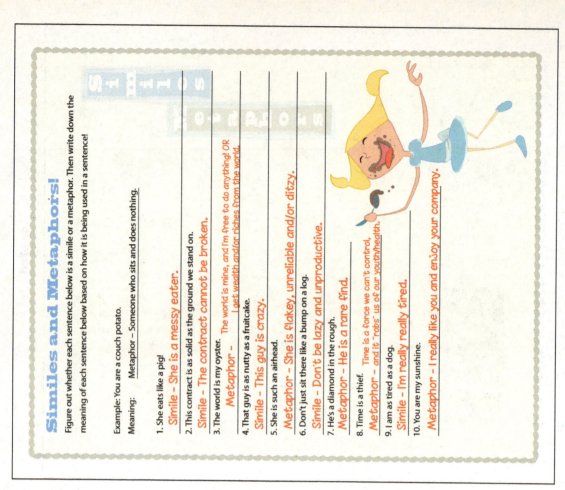

page 41

ASSONANCE AND CONSONANCE

Assonance and consonance are often used together. Read the quotes below and figure out where assonance and/or consonance are being used. Then write down what sounds are being repeated.

EXAMPLE: Or hear old Triton blow his wreathed horn.   o-Assonance

1. From the molten golden notes, (o)-A, (en)-C

2. Her finger hungered for a ring. (ng), (er)-C

3. Cupid laid by his brand. (i)-A

4. How they clang, and clash, (a)-A

5. and roar! What a horror they outpour. (or sound)-C

6. Whose woods these are I think I know. (s)-C

7. He saw the cost and hauled off. (awe sound)-A

8. Gayle tapped a finger on the sack of books in her lap. (a)-A

9. I sipped the rim with palatable lip. (i)-A

10. A gallant knight, in sunshine and in shadow, (a)-A

11. "Thou art a fool," said my head to my heart. (a)-A, (rt)-C

12. What a world of merriment their melody foretells! (r)-C

13. It was half as funny after, when they laughed so at the staff. (aff sound)-C

14. Well that was short but sweet. (t)-C

ONOMATOPOEIA

An **onomatopoeia** (pronounced: on-oh-mat-oh-PEA-uh) is a word that imitates the sound that it describes.

Word bank: quack, pop, tick, roar, bark, snap, chatter, swish, crackle, bang, screech, sizzle, click, chirp, buzz

Choose a word from the word bank to help complete the sentences.

1. The bird loved to **chirp** a merry tune.

2. The **tick** of the clock kept me up all night.

3. The food on the stove made a nice **sizzle**.

4. She kept making a **click** noise with her pen and it drove the teacher crazy!

5. The little dogs like to **bark** at the cat.

6. Something upset the lion and it made a loud **roar**.

7. I heard the ruler **snap** against the desk.

8. His teeth started to **chatter** outside in the cold.

9. The fire made a **crackle** when they added more wood.

10. As the car started up it made a loud **bang**.

11. The chalk **screeched** on the black board.

12. The wheel went **pop** as we ran over a nail in the road.

13. The ducklings **quacked** behind their mother.

14. Her dress makes a **swish** noise as she walks.

15. The bees happily **buzz** around the garden.

Vocabulary Practice

Peter Pan
J.M.Barrie

Answer the vocabulary questions below and refer back to the text as needed.

Part 1

Definitions

Write the letter in the blank space next to the correct definition.

a. consulting — **f** — to take up all of your attention

b. implicitly — **e** — sharing the same feeling

c. contempt — **b** — without question

d. disturb — **d** — bother or trouble

e. mutual — **a** — to check for advice or information

f. engrossed — **c** — to have negative feelings towards something or someone

Find a word in the text that means:

happy — **gaily**   scared — **with horror**

tired — **sleepy**   bad — **awful**

Vocabulary Practice

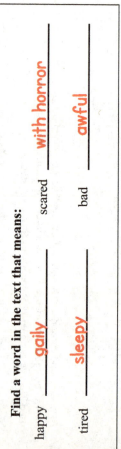

Peter Pan
J.M.Barrie

Answer the vocabulary questions below and refer back to the text as needed.

Part 2

Definitions

Write the letter in the blank space next to the correct definition.

a. polite — **c** — to help someone remember

b. impressed — **e** — thin, overlapping plates

c. reminded — **b** — to emphasize or urge something

d. constantly — **f** — to be annoying

e. scales — **d** — something happening over and over

f. irritating — **a** — showing good manners towards others

What do you think?

In your own words, write definitions for the following:

• fearfully

• mermaid

Vocabulary Practice

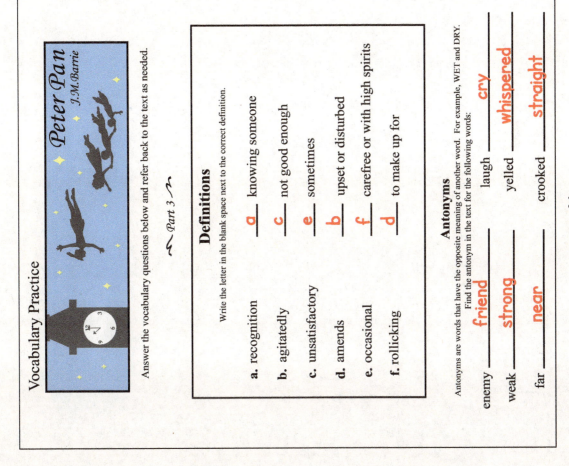

Peter Pan
J.M.Barrie

Answer the vocabulary questions below and refer back to the text as needed.

~ *Part 3* ~

Definitions

Write the letter in the blank space next to the correct definition.

a. recognition

b. agitatedly

c. unsatisfactory

d. amends

e. occasional

f. rollicking

a   knowing someone

c   not good enough

e   sometimes

b   upset or disturbed

f   carefree or with high spirits

d   to make up for

Antonyms

Antonyms are words that have the opposite meaning of another word. For example, WET and DRY.
Find the antonym in the text for the following words:

enemy	**friend**	laugh	**cry**
weak	**strong**	yelled	**whispered**
far	**near**	crooked	**straight**

page 64